LESSONS FROM HISTORY
A Celebration in Blackness

Elementary Edition

by Jawanza Kunjufu

Illustrated by Yaounde Olu and Cornell Barnes

Chicago, Illinois

Photo Credits
Argonne Laboratory
Final Call
NASA
Vivian Harsh Collection
William Hall

Cover Illustration by Yaounde Olu

First Edition
Thirteenth Printing

Dedication

To Mrs. Avery, Hudson, Allen, Butler, Foote, Marks, Mr. Payne, Boughton, and Richards, all Black teachers who taught me Black history by being positive role models, who demanded excellence.

To African American children who deserve more than Negro history, which gives them only one day of lessons about Africa, two days of lessons on the slaveship, and the remainder of the course being slavery or fighting racism in America, Negro history —all taught in February, the shortest month of the year.

To Carol Finn, who just happens to be a White principal of African American children, who inspired me to write this textbook. I had planned to write *Lessons from History* in 1988 as a story book. She reminded me that there are few comprehensive Black history textbooks in print for the elementary and junior high school student.

Special Thanks

Special thanks is given to Kawana Sherman, Janice Crayton, Mary Lewis, Yolanda Taylor, and Mary Brown for their editorial assistance. A special thanks is given to Sanyika Anwisye who spent long hours with me editing and rewriting the manuscript, lastly, my family that went without a husband and father many days, but encouraged me to continue.

Table of Contents

Preface

In this book Black people will be called Africans or African Americans. Why? Because Black people wherever they are, come from the *land* called Africa. We have been called by many different names—colored, Negro, Black, etc. Most people are known by the land which they or their ancestors lived in or come from. Germans are called Germans because there is a land named Germany. Irish are called Irish because there is a land named Ireland. Chinese are called Chinese because there is a land called China. Mexicans are called Mexicans because there is a land named Mexico. Now look at the map. Is there a place called Colorland? Negroland? Blackland? No. There is a land named Africa, which is where we came from. So, in our book, we shall refer to ourselves as Africans, African Americans, and Africans in America.

Chapter One
Africa, The Beginning of Civilization

Africa has a land area of twelve million square miles.
Africa is the second largest continent.
Africa is almost three times the size of America.
Most maps show them being equal in size. Africa is in the tropics and is very warm.

Africa is the birthplace of humanity.
The original man was in Ethiopia.
Africans lived almost 4 million years ago.
Asians lived over 700 thousand years ago.
Europeans lived over 70 thousand years ago.

There are many pyramids in Egypt.
Imhotep drew the plans for the first pyramid.
The pyramids of Gizeh are the largest.
One is 48 stories high and 755 feet wide.

The pyramids were built almost five thousand years ago.
It took sixty years to finish them.
Africans also built large temples and tombs, that still stand today.
Africans were the first to make laws for mathematics and science.
Imhotep was the father of medicine.

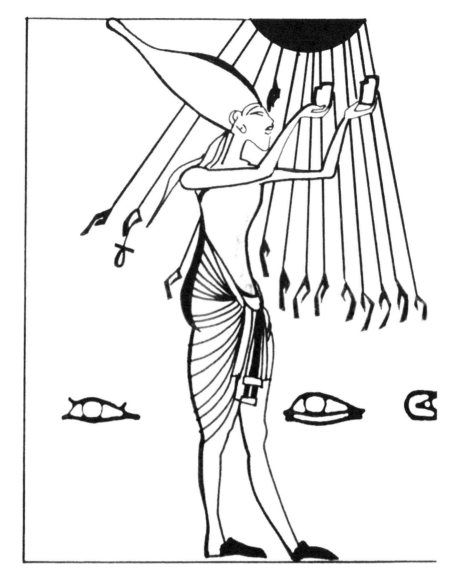

Africans wrote with pictures, called hie-ro-gly-phics. Some people call this period prehistory because they did not know how to write. Africans call it history because we could write.
Africans founded the first university.
It was called the Grand Lodge of Wa'at.
Greeks and Romans learned from the Egyptians.
The buildings remain in the city called Luxor.

Africans had great kings and queens.
Some of the Kings were Akhenaten, Tutankhamon
(Tut), and Ramses.
Some of the queens were N'Zinga, Hatshepsut, and
Nefertiti. The kings and queens respected each oth-
er.

The beginning of religion was in Africa.
The ankh is the sign of life.
The cross is shaped almost like the ankh.
Many Africans believed in one God, Amon-Ra.
There may be a relationship between ending prayers with Amen and the African God Amon-Ra.

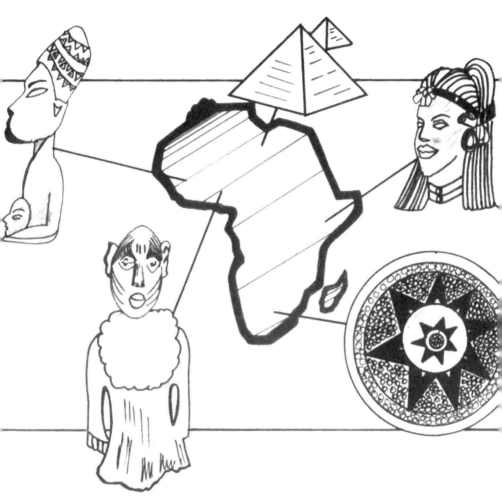

Africans lived all over the continent.
We lived in the north, south, east, and west.
Some of the countries are Egypt, Azania, Kenya, and Nigeria.
Africans built the great empires of Ghana, Mali, and Songhay. A few of the communities are the Masai, Ashanti, Yoruba, Zulu, and Nubians.

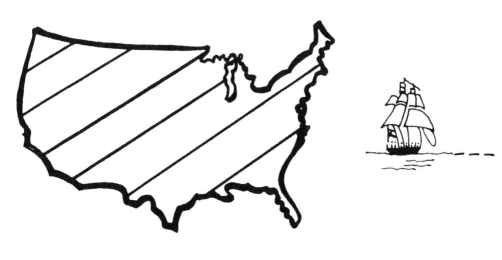

Africans were great travelers.
They had been to America over three thousand years before Columbus.
Africans also sailed to Asia and Europe.
We were master shipbuilders.

Africa is a very rich land.
It has gold, diamonds, and many other natural resources.
The land is full of plants and trees bearing food.
Other countries need African resources to survive and grow.

Modern Africa is very different from what we've seen on television.

It has large cities, hotels, office buildings, and cars.

It also has country farms, roads, and animals.

The food shortage is a result of large amounts of land becoming a desert.

There are about 500 million people in Africa.

Bibliography

Children

Ancient African Kingdom. Golden Legacy History Magazine, Seattle: Baylor Publisher, 1983.

Educational Coloring Books. African History, Houston: Aka Publications.

Jefferson, Cynthia. *My Calendar Book.* Buffalo: St. Augustine Center, 1982.

Musgrove, Margaret. *Ashanti to Zulu.* New York: New American Library, 1976.

Sibbett, Ed, Jr. *Ancient Egyptian Design.* New York: Dover, 1978.

Adult

Carruthers, Jacob. *Essays in Ancient Egyptian Studies.* Los Angeles: University of Sankore Press, 1984.

Diop, Cheikh Anta. *The African Origin of Civilization.* New York: Lawrence Hill, 1974.

_____. *The Cultural Unity of Black Africa.* Chicago: Third World Press, 1978.

Hilliard, Asa. *From Ancient Africa to African-American Today.* Portland: Portland Public Schools, 1983.

Jackson, John. *Man God and Civilization.* Secaucus: Citadel Press, 1972.

James, George. *Stolen Legacy.* San Francisco: Julian Richardson, 1976.

Jochannon, Yosef Ben. *African Origins of the Major Western Religions.* New York: Alkebu-lan, 1970.

_____. *Black Man of the Nile.* New York: Alkebu-lan, 1981.

Kush, Indus Khamit. *What They Never Told You in History Class.* New York: Luxorr Publication, 1983.

Sertima, Ivan Van. *They Came Before Columbus.* New York: Random House, 1976.

Williams, Chancellor. *Destruction of Black Civilization.* Chicago: Third World Press, 1974.

Vocabulary
Write the definition of each word.
Write a sentence using each word.

Draw a picture of your favorite word on the list or in the chapter.

continent	resource
empire	rich
location	sign
master	survive
prehistory	temple
produce	tomb
pyramid	university
religion	

Questions

1) How large is Africa?
2) Which is larger, America or Africa?
3) Where was the first man found?
4) Describe the pyramid of Gizeh.
5) What is the ankh?
6) Who was Imhotep?
7) What was the first university?
8) Who learned from the Egyptians?
9) Name a king and queen.
10) Name three great African empires.
11) What are two natural resources found in Africa?
12) Who arrived in America first, Columbus or Africans?
13) About how many people live in Africa?

Exercises

1) Draw a map of Africa and draw a picture of your family inside.
2) Draw a map of Africa and decorate it with pictures cut from a magazine.
3) Draw a map of Africa and draw a pyramid on the inside. Write Imhotep on the pyramid.
4) Draw an ankh and a cross.
5) Tape on construction paper something gold, silver, and copper. Teacher can show a diamond.
6) Watch a movie of Africa that shows the great pyramids, temples, empires, universities, its abundant natural resources, and its modern facilities — avoid Tarzan movies unless you show it for its contradictions.

12

Chapter Two

The Invaders

There were many people who invaded Africa. They included Asians, Arabs, Greeks, Romans, and Northern Europeans. Africans welcomed them to their land. They provided them with food, water, and a tour of the area. Africans treated them as visitors and friends.

These people had come from places that were
cold and with few resources. They enjoyed the
warm air, fruit on the vine, and gold in the mines.
They also saw how nice Africans treated them.
They met, decided to take the land, and over a period of years made Africans slaves.

Africans had used iron for their buildings. They
made carbon steel in mud ovens. These invaders
used iron for swords, knives, arrows, and guns. The
Africans only had spears and shields and a few
knives.

The invaders saw a large rich land, with people all over and in small separate groups. The invaders had two advantages: the gun and unity.

*   *   *   *   *

Africans were brave and fought back with their limited weapons. Some kings bought guns, but force, trickery, and greed made them trade their people for guns.

These people were taken to the coast next to the water. One place was called Goree Island in West Africa. It was the last time many of them would see Africa. The invaders and the Africans kept fighting.

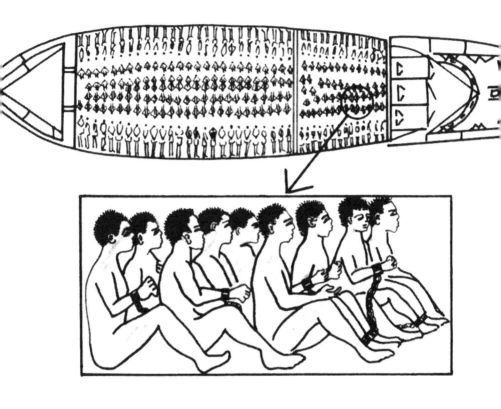

The Africans were placed in boats like animals. They were forced to lay chained next to each other. There was no room to move legs or arms. The trip lasted two months. Many died before arriving in North, South, and Central America. The exact number is not certain, but around 100 million Africans died throughout slavery.

Africans did not accept slavery. There were many fights on the boats. Many Africans jumped off the boat. Some Africans chose not to eat, rather than be a slave in America. It was hard to fight when your hands and legs were chained. Joseph Cinque led a takeover of the *Amistad* ship, and eventually returned back to Africa.

Before Africans were sold to owners, they had to be "seasoned." In seasoning, slave makers would beat the slaves until Africans believed these rules: To be afraid of the owner and possible death for disobeying. To identify and be loyal to the owner. To believe the White race is superior to the Black race. To hate Africa and anything Black.

The Africans were sold like objects. "Who will pay $500 dollars for this strong colored Mandingo? Sold for $500 dollars! Who will pay $500 for this strong colored girl who can make more slaves? Sold for $500 dollars!"

The Africans tried to stay together, but owners sold fathers to other owners in one state, mothers to another, and the children somewhere else. African husbands, wives, and children hugged each other and cried when they were separated. Slavery has always existed. Africans and all the other races enslaved people. However, this slavery from the Arabs and Europeans was the most brutal in history.

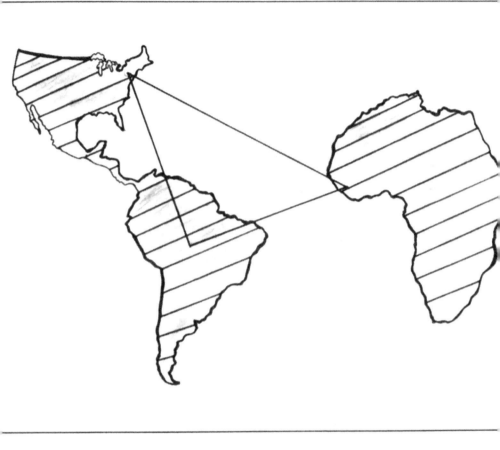

Africans were brought to many countries including Brazil, Haiti, and the United States. Most of the Africans worked in the fields. Some of the crops grown were cotton, sugar and tobacco. They worked from sunrise to sunset.

A few Africans worked in the owner's house. They worked hard, but not as hard as those who worked in the fields. These Africans were many times lighter-skinned. They had White fathers and Black mothers. Some loved their fathers and hated their mothers, while others hated their father and loved their mother.

After working from sunrise to sunset some Africans would read under a candle or the moonlight. They had to hide while reading, because the owner was not in favor of slaves being educated.

From Africa, on the boat, to the plantation, Africans never accepted slavery. To resist slavery, they worked slowly on purpose, broke tools, and set fires to the crops. There were over 265 slave revolts. They were led by people like Nat Turner, Denmark Vesey, Gabriel Prosser, and Harriet Tubman.

Harriet Tubman brought 300 African Americans North to freedom. She went South 19 times with the help of the Underground Railroad. The Underground Railroad was a two hundred mile journey following the North Star. Some Whites helped by providing housing and hiding places.

John Brown, a White man, also spoke against
slavery and led a slave revolt at Harper's Ferry.
Free African-Americans spoke around the country,
hoping to get more Whites to end slavery. Frederick Douglass was one of the best speakers and writers.

The North and South could not agree. The North wanted Africans to work in their factories for low wages. The South wanted Africans to be slaves on the plantations. Abraham Lincoln signed the Emancipation Proclamation, allowing Africans in the South to fight with the North and help them win. It did not free Africans in northern states. Lincoln felt Africans were inferior and considered sending them to Liberia in West Africa.

Bibliography

Children
Joseph Cinque and the Amistad Mutiny.
Frederick Douglass.
The Saga of Harriet Tubman. Golden Legacy Magazines, Seattle:
  Baylor Publishing, 1983.

Adult
Bennett, Lerone. *Before the Mayflower.* Chicago: Johnson Pub-
  lishing, 1962.
Gutman, Herbert. *The Black Family in Slavery and Freedom.*
  New York: Vintage, 1976.
Harding, Vincent. *There is a River.* New York: Harcourt Brace
  Jovanovich, 1981.

Vocabulary

Write the definition of each word. Write a sentence using each
word. Draw a picture of your favorite word on the list or in the
chapter.

accept	object
advantages	plan
area	plantation
brave	revolt
coast	shield
crop	slave
divide	spear
exact	takeover
field	trade
gun	travel
invader	unity
island	value

Questions

1) How did Africans treat their visitors?
2) Compare the minerals of Europe and Africa.
3) How were Europeans able to defeat Africans?
4) Why did some African kings sell their people?
5) What was the last stop for many Africans before leaving?

6) Describe slavery on the boat.
7) What did Joseph Cinque do?
8) What happened to the African family during slavery?
9) What were some of the major crops during slavery?
10) How did some Africans become lighter-skinned?
11) Is your desire to read as great as Africans who read under candlelight?
12) How many slave revolts were made?
13) How did Abraham Lincoln feel about Africans?

Exercises

1) With enough index cards for all students, mark half of them "owner," and half "slave" and let each student select a card. The owners will boss the slaves for that day. The next day, reverse the relationship.
2) Design a family tree chart and have the students fill in with parental help as many generations as possible.
3) Tape on construction paper, cotton, tobacco, and a sugar cube.

Chapter Three

The Search for Liberation

African churches began celebrating "Watch Meeting Services" December 31, 1862. The ritual of bringing in the new year was a special occasion. The Emancipation Proclamation which became a law January 1, 1863, allowed Africans in the South to fight with the North. It did not end slavery. Many churches still celebrate "Watch Meeting Services" on New Year's Eve.

The slaves were free to do what? To go where? How? Martin Delany explored the return to Africa. Frederick Douglass said, "If there is no struggle, there is no progress."

Booker T. Washington said, "No race can grow until it learns that there is as much dignity in tilling a field as in writing a poem."

W.E.B. DuBois said, "The problem of the twentieth century is the problem of color."

Africans have always been concerned with government. After slavery, African Americans were elected to local, state, and national offices. Hiram Revels and Blanche Bruce were senators from Mississippi. Today, there are over twenty African American Congresspersons, over one hundred mayors, and over five thousand other elected officials.

The South was not used to Africans having power. The South was angry at the North for giving them positions. The North did not enforce the new laws and let the South decide what to do with African Americans. Africans lost their positions and many were killed during the period of 1890-1920.

Millions of Africans left the South going North. Most went by train. Africans followed the direction of the railroad tracks. Those living in the Carolinas and Georgia went to New York, Philadelphia, Baltimore, and Washington. Those living in Mississippi, Alabama, and Tennessee arrived in Chicago, Detroit, Cleveland, and St. Louis. Those living in Arkansas, Texas, and Oklahoma traveled to California.

When African Americans moved to New York, they moved into a community called Harlem. City life was very different from the plantation. Africans still worked very hard in the factories for low wages and many could not find work, but they endured by expressing their many talents. The Harlem Renaissance showed the world some of the best talent in music, singing, dancing, writing, and art.

Marcus Garvey was one of the greatest African leaders. Booker T. Washington invited him to America from Jamaica. Marcus Garvey organized over one million African Americans to believe "Black is beautiful" and "Africa for the Africans." His group, called the Universal Negro Improvement Association (UNIA), owned stores, ships, and newspapers.

Elijah Muhammad worked with Marcus Garvey. Mr. Muhammad founded the Nation of Islam. He taught African-Americans to feel good about their race, and start their own businesses. The Muslims also owned stores, newspapers, schools, and farms.

It was December 1, 1955. Rosa Parks had worked another long hard day when she boarded a bus in Montgomery, Alabama. She sat down in the front of the bus. Blacks were supposed to move to the back when Whites wanted to sit down. The bus began to fill with Blacks and Whites. When a White man wanted to sit down in Mrs. Parks' seat, she refused to move and was arrested.

Dr. Martin Luther King, Jr. was asked by African Americans in Montgomery to lead them. They decided if African Americans could not sit where they wanted, they would rather walk and keep their money. This is called a boycott — you refuse to support a business until you receive fairness. The boycott lasted 381 days, until African Americans won. They could now sit anywhere on the bus.

There were many "Jim Crow" laws that African Americans wanted to change. There were separate toilets, water fountains, parks, schools, theatres, and restaurants for Blacks and Whites. There were Africans, Whites, and groups that boycotted, marched, and were beaten so that we could be free. Martin Luther King, Jr. won the Nobel Peace Prize in 1964, because he felt freedom could be won with peace. Dr. King's love for justice was greater than his fear of death.

Malcolm X was many things. He began as a criminal and prisoner, but became a student, organizer, minister, and world leader. Malcolm was a Muslim minister for the Nation of Islam. He was a very good speaker and drew crowds the size of Marcus Garvey's. Malcolm X taught racial pride, economics, and self-defense. Some people say King's programs were aided by the fear Whites had for Malcolm's program.

Rev. Jesse Jackson was a follower of Dr. King. Louis Farrakhan was a follower of Elijah Muhammad. Many people try to separate King from Malcolm, Jackson from Farrakhan, Douglass from Delany. They want Africans to make choices, but give more information about Jackson, King, and Douglass. Douglass, King, and Jackson believed in boycotts, marches, non-violence, and equal opportunity. Delany, Garvey, Muhammad, Malcolm X, and Farrakhan believed in owning businesses, land, schools, and self-defense. We like all of them because they all want Africans to be free. We should rely more on the *message* than the *messenger*, because messengers die.

The struggle for freedom remains in Azania
(South Africa). Four million Europeans have control over twenty-two million Africans. The Whites
have the best of all resources and they force Africans to live on the poorest land. The Whites have
more and better guns. This form of slavery is called
apartheid. Nelson and Winnie Mandela, Bishop
Desmond Tutu, Oliver Tambo, and many groups
lead Africans in their drive for freedom.

Bibliography

Children

The Life of Martin Luther King. Golden Legacy Magazine, Seattle: Baylor Publishing, 1983.

Adoff, Arnold. *Malcolm X.* New York: Harper & Row, 1970.

Dennis, Denise. *Black History for Beginners.* New York: Writers and Readers Publishings, 1984.

Giles, Lucille. *Color Me Brown.* Chicago: Johnson Publishing, 1976.

Taifa, Nkechi. *Shining Legacy.* Washington: House of Songhay II, 1983.

Adult

Adams, Russell. *Great Negroes Past and Present.* Chicago: Afro-Am Publishing, 1963.

Banks, James, *March Toward Freedom.* Belmont: Fearon Pittman Publishers, 1978.

Bell, Janet. *Famous Black Quotations.* Chicago: Sabayt Publications, 1986.

Davis, Allison. *Leadership, Love and Aggression.* New York: Harcourt, 1983.

Franklin, John Hope. *From Slavery To Freedom.* New York: Knopf, 1947.

Muhammad, Elijah. *Message to the Blackman.* Chicago: Muhammad Mosque, 1965.

X, Malcolm. *Autobiography of Malcolm X.* New York: Grove, 1964.

Vocabulary

Write the definition of each word. Write a sentence using each word. Draw a picture of your favorite word on the list or in the chapter.

boycott	mayor
bus	office
business	peace
century	period
choice	poem
civil	power
defense	proclamation
dignity	race
elect	senator

founded   ship
freedom   shop
government   struggle
leader   tower
local

Questions

1) What is the Watch Meeting Service?
2) How many African American elected officials are there today?
3) How did the South react to the end of slavery?
4) Why didn't Africans living in South Carolina move to California?
5) What was the Harlem Renaissance?
6) Who was Marcus Garvey?
7) What did Elijah Muhammad teach Africans?
8) What is a boycott?
9) What did Doctor King believe?
10) List the things Malcolm X did.
11) What did Doctor King and Malcolm X have in common?
12) What is happening in Azania (South Africa)?

Exercises

1) Write a paper imagining you were just made free. Where would you go? What would you do? What do you own?
2) Write a poem as if you were Rosa Parks, the day she did not move to the back of the bus.
3) Draw a picture of African Americans taking a train to the North.

Chapter Four

We Call Them Brave

King Ramses (1328-1232 B.C. est.)

King Ramses II was a very great king. He ruled Egypt for 66 years. The Hittites invaded Egypt, but King Ramses directed his army to victory. Under his leadership, more temples, tombs and pyramids were built than under any other king. King Ramses kept Egypt safe for a long time.

47

Hannibal (247-183 B.C.)

Hannibal was a great military hero. He led the Carthage army against the Roman invaders. Hannibal was outnumbered many times in battle, but outsmarted the enemy. His greatest victory against the Romans was achieved with his 32,000 versus 90,000 Romans.

Queen N'Zinga (1582-1663)

Queen N'Zinga wanted to stop slavery. In her home, Angola, she fought the Portuguese for over forty years. She was very smart and brave. Queen N'Zinga's troops would attack quickly and hide, and place spies in the enemy's army.

Toussaint L'Ouverture (1746-1803)

Toussaint L'Ouverture was born a slave, but became general and governor of Santa Domingo at a young age. Toussaint was taught reading and other skills by his father and godfather. The island of Haiti was desired by many European nations. L'Ouverture led the Africans against all of them and won every battle. He made a mistake with France, by trusting them, and they took him as a prisoner. Jacques Dessalines, his second general, eventually won against France.

Chaka Zulu (1786-1836)

Chaka showed great courage as a boy by killing a snake and a leopard. At age 26, he became chief of the Zulu community. He is often called Chaka Zulu or the Great Elephant. Chaka's troops had used special attacks to prevent the British and Dutch from taking Azania (South Africa).

Joseph Cinque (1811-1879)

Cinque was born a prince in Africa. The invaders caught him and tried to take him to America. Aboard the ship, named the *Amistad*, Cinque and other Africans planned a takeover. Cinque and others were successful, but were eventually caught by another ship. Two years later and after many court trials, the judge ruled that Cinque and thirty-five African survivors were free to return home to Africa.

Denmark Vesey (1767-1822)

Vesey was born a slave, bought his freedom, and became a wealthy carpenter and minister. Vesey heard about Toussaint's victory in Haiti, and wanted Africans in America to also be free. Vesey organized 9,000 African Americans to plan a slave revolt in South Carolina. He planned for two years, but a "traitor" told the plan to Whites. As a result, Vesey and thirty-four African Americans were hung.

Harriet Tubman (1820 est.-1913)

At the young age of fourteen, Harriet began her mission of freeing slaves. She jumped between an owner throwing a brick at an African who was trying to run away. Later, she ran away and followed the North Star to Philadelphia. Concerned about all the other Africans in slavery, she returned to the South nineteen times and freed 300 people. During the Civil War she served as a scout and nurse.

Nat Love ("Deadwood Dick") (1856-1900)

Often "his-story" and television programs leave out African Americans. There were over 5,000 African cowboys who blazed the western trails. One of the best was Nat Love, nicknamed "Deadwood Dick" because of his skillful shooting. Deadwood Dick was one of the best horse riders, cattle herders and fighters the West has ever seen. Nat Love not only won shooting contests, but also at the rodeo, roping the wildest mustang horse.

Muhammad Ali (Cassius Clay) (1941-)

A good fighter fights with his body, mind, and soul. Cassius Clay won the Golden Gloves championship in 1959, the Olympics in 1960, and the heavyweight championship in 1964. He became a Muslim in 1964, changed his name to Muhammad Ali, and became a fighter for African liberation. He refused to fight in the Vietnam War because of his religion. Then his title was taken from him, he was sent to jail, and bad things were said about him. Three years later in 1970, the court allowed him to fight again and Muhammad Ali went on to become the champion two more times.

America has had many wars: the Revolutionary, 1812, Civil, Spanish American, World War I and II, Korean, and Vietnam. African Americans have always hoped that fighting for freedom abroad would help America give them freedom at home. There were 5,000 Africans who fought in the Revolutionary War, where Crispus Attucks was the first to die. Before World War I, African Americans were only used when Whites saw no other way to win.

From World War I to the present, African Americans have been used more on the front line where they are more likely to be injured or killed. Meanwhile the Klu Klux Klan hid behind sheets, fighting only when the numbers were on their side. The Tuskegee Airmen, made of 600 World War II pilots, destroyed 261 planes and received eighty-two awards of courage. The movie *Platoon* does not show the bravery nor the large numbers of Africans who died in Vietnam. We must fight for freedom for ourselves, before we fight for freedom for others.

Bibliography

Children

Black Cowboys.

The Saga of Toussaint L' Ouverture.

Crispus Attacks. Golden Legacy Magazine, Seattle: Baylor Publishing, 1983.

Olomenji. *Great Black Military Heroes.* Chicago: New Frontiers Unlimited Press, 1983.

Adult

Ali, Muhammad. *The Greatest, My Own Story.* New York: Random House, 1975.

Vocabulary

Write the definition of each word. Write a sentence using each word. Draw a picture of your favorite word on the list or in the chapter.

aboard	king
abroad	military
against	pilot
army	prevent
attack	prisoner
battle	return
cattle	rodeo
champion	safe
chief	scout
courage	skill
die	spy
directed	trails
enemy	trial
general	versus
hero	victory

Questions

1) How long did King Ramses lead Egypt?
2) What made King Ramses great?
3) Why was Hannibal a great military hero?
4) What mistake did Toussaint L'Ouverture make?
5) What happened to Denmark Vesey's revolt?
6) What made Harriet Tubman special?

7) Why was Nat Love called Deadwood Dick?
8) Describe the Tuskegee Airmen.
9) What was N'Zinga's plan?
10) What made Muhammad Ali brave?

Exercises

1) Draw a picture of your favorite person in this Chapter.
2) Form a circle, and act out Muhammad Ali's chant, "Float like a butterfly, sting like a bee."

Chapter Five

The African Contribution

Africans have always been good in science, from Imhotep to Ben Carson, from the lawn mower, stove and refrigerator, to the fountain pen and pencil sharpener. The slogan "The Real McCoy" is in honor of Elijah McCoy. Almost everything we touch, African American inventors made a contribution.

When someone invents something, they should get a patent to protect their idea from people who want to steal it. Slaves were not allowed to get patents. After slavery, many Africans could not afford to pay for a patent. Many Africans could not afford to start their own businesses to manufacture and sell their inventions. Many Whites took African inventors' ideas or paid them very little for their inventions.

Imhotep (3,000 B.C. - 2920 B.C. est.)

Imhotep is the father of medicine. Medical students take an oath in his honor. He was also the designer of the first pyramid. Imhotep was a great doctor and was involved in preparing mummies. Mummies are dead bodies that are preserved.

Benjamin Banneker (1731-1806)

Benjamin Banneker took a watch apart, studied it, and made the first clock. Banneker studied the stars and weather patterns and wrote an almanac to help farmers. In designing Washington D.C., Banneker had to remember the plans in his head. Banneker said, "The color of the skin is in no way connected with the strength of the mind."

Jan Matzeliger (1852-1889)

Take a look at your shoe and thank Jan Matzeliger. Before Matzeliger invented his shoe lasting machine, the upper shoe and sole were sewn by hand. Matzeliger made a machine that would automatically sew the two parts together. This created a large industry of shoe companies.

Granville Woods (1856-1910)

Alexander Bell and Thomas Edison owe much to Granville Woods. The first telephone could barely be heard and not over long distances. Woods invented a transmitter that improved the hearing over greater distances. Woods also invented the "third rail" for the train system, and other electrical devices that Edison said were his.

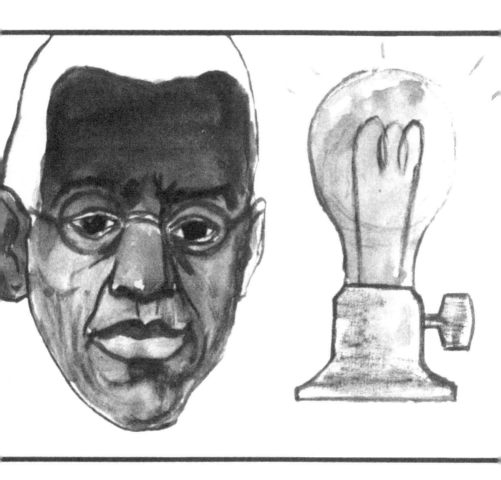

Lewis Latimer (1848-1928)

Bell and Edison also owe much to Lewis Latimer. Latimer drew the plans for Bell's telephone. Latimer worked for Edison and defended him in court, and saved him millions of dollars. Latimer improved the making of carbon filaments used in light bulbs. This allowed them to last longer.

Garrett Morgan (1867-1963)

Stop at the red light, thanks to Garrett Morgan. This invention reduced many accidents and made traffic orderly. Morgan also made the breathing mask for firefighters. Many firefighters were being hurt because they had no masks. With the help of Garrett Morgan, we can drive safely and firefighters can save lives.

George Washington Carver (1864-1943)

Do you know what is inside a peanut or sweet potato? George Washington Carver found oils that were used for soap, shampoo, ink, and 300 other products. The South grew rich off his ideas, including changing the crops to enrich the soil. Carver was also a professor at Tuskegee Institute, founded by Booker T. Washington.

Dr. Mae Jemison (1956 -)

Mae is the first African American female to become an astronaut. She is an engineer and a doctor. As a student, she earned excellent grades in science, math, and computers. Her outstanding achievements allowed her to study and provide health care in Cuba, Kenya, Liberia, and other countries. In 1987, NASA selected her for their astronaut training program. Dr. Jemison is qualified to serve as a mission specialist on Space Shuttle flight crews.

Dr. Ben Carson (1951 -)

Dr. Carson is a pediatric surgeon. He performs surgery on children who have brain disorders. As a child, he was deeply interested in animals, nature, and science. In 1987, Dr. Carson performed the first successful separation of Siamese twins who were joined at the back of the head. This delicate and difficult operation required five months of planning and 22 hours of surgery.

Children

The Black Inventors Latimer and Woods.

The life of Benjamin Banneker. Golden Legacy Magazine, Seattle: Baylor Publishing, 1983.

Carson, Ben and Cecil Murphey. *Gifted Hands: The Ben Carson Story.* Grand Rapids: Zonderan Publishing House, 1990.

Winslow, Eugene. *Black Americans in Science and Engineering.* Chicago: Afro-Am Publishing, 1974.

Adult

A Salute to Black Scientists and Inventors. Chicago: Empak Enterprises, 1985.

Carwell, Hattie. *Blacks in Science.* Hicksville: Exposition Press, 1977.

Vocabulary

Write the definition of each word. Write a sentence using each word. Draw a picture of your favorite word on the list or in the chapter.

clock	mummies	soap
engineer	patent	soil
idea	peanut	stars
ink	physics	telephone
inventor	science	ton
mask	shoe	transmitter
mechanical		

Questions

1) List some African inventions.
2) How was Alexander Bell helped by African Americans?
3) How was Edison helped by Lewis Latimer?
4) Who was the father of medicine?
5) Why was it difficult for African Americans to use their inventions?
6) Who designed Washington, D.C.
7) Describe the work of George Washington Carver?
8) Who was the first African American female to become an astronaut?

Exercises

1) Bring in as many items invented by African Americans as you can.
2) Connect your school science project to this chapter.

Chapter Six
African Culture

Culture is more than music, art, language, and food. It is everything you do. Culture is your value system and world view. Africans believe in harmony with people, animals, water, land, and air. Africans believe "Hofu Ni Kwenu," my concern is for you.

Nguzo Saba African Value System

UMOJA (Unity)
To strive for and maintain unity in the family, community, nation, and race.

KUJICHAGULIA (Self-determination)
To define ourselves, name ourselves, create for ourselves and speak for ourselves instead of being defined, named, created for and spoken for by others.

UJIMA (Collective Work and Responsibility)
To build and maintain our community together and make our sister's and brother's problems our problems, and to solve them together.

UJAMAA (Cooperative Economics)
To build and maintain our own stores, shops, and other businesses, and to profit from them together.

NIA (Purpose)
To make our collective vocation the building and developing of our community in order to restore our people to their traditional greatness.

KUUMBA (Creativity)
To do always as much as we can, in the way we can, in order to leave our community more beautiful and beneficial than we inherited it.

IMANI (Faith)
To believe with all our heart in our people, our parents, our teachers, our leaders and the righteousness and victory of our struggle.

Africans were the first to believe in one God. Africans also believe in life after death. The church is a major part of culture. Africans in slavery prayed to God for a better day, "by and by."

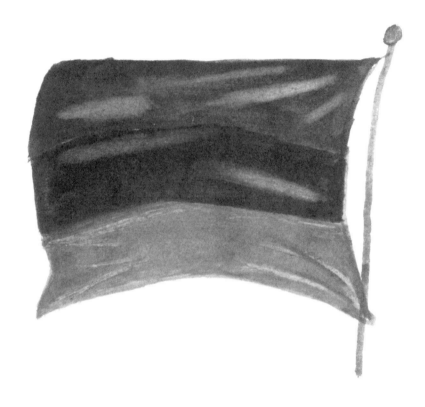

This is the liberation flag. The creator of the flag is Marcus Garvey. Red stands for the blood and struggle. Black stands for the people and color. Green stands for land and the future.

Allegiance of the Flag (U.N.I.A.)

This flag IS Mine
Here's to this flag of mine,
the Red, Black, and Green
Hopes in its future bright
Africa has seen.

Here's to the Red of it,
Great Nations shall know of it
In time to come.
Red blood shall flow of it.
Great flag of mine.

Here's to the Black of it
Four hundred millions back of it.
Whose destiny depends on it
The Red, Black, and Green of it.
Oh, flag of mine.

Here's to the Green of it
Young men shall dream of it,
Face shot and shells of it,
Maidens shall sing of it
Waving so high.

Here's to the whole of it
Colors brought and pole of it
Pleased is my soul with it
Regardless of what is told of it,
Thanks God for giving it
Great flag of mine.

"Lift Every Voice and Sing"
James Weldon Johnson

Lift every voice and sing, till earth and heaven ring,
Ring with the harmonies of liberty;
Let our rejoicing rise, high as the listening skies,
Let it resound loud as the rolling sea.

Sing a song full of the faith that the dark past has
   taught us,
Sing a song full of the hope that the present has
   brought us;
Facing the rising sun of our new day begun,
Let us march on till victory is won.

Stony the road we trod, bitter the chastening rod,
Felt in the days when hope unborn had died;
Yet with a steady beat, have not our weary feet,
Come to the place for which our fathers sighed?
We have come over a way that with tears has been
   watered,
We have come, treading our path through the blood
   of the slaughtered,
Out from the gloomy past, till now we stand at
   last,
Where the white gleam of our bright star is cast.

God of our weary years, God of our silent tears,
Thou who hast brought us thus far on the way;
Thou who has by Thy might, led us into the light,
Keep us forever in the path, we pray.
Lest our feet stray from the places, our God, where
   we met Thee,
Lest our hearts, drunk with the wine of the world,
   we forget Thee;
Shadowed beneath Thy hand, may we forever
   stand,
True to our God, true to our native land.

There were many communities in Africa, including Yoruba, Ashanti, Masai, and Zulu. Africans spoke over 2,000 languages. The slave owner did not allow Africans to speak their home or native language. He made them speak English, so he could understand what was said.

Swahili was selected in 1974 by members of the Pan-African conference as the Pan-African language. This will allow Africans living all over the world to understand each other.

Listed below is a working Swahili vocabulary.

Phonics

a - short a
e - long a
i - long e
o - long o
u - long u

Common Words

Jambo	Hello
Habari Gani	What is the news
Njema	Fine
Asante	Thank you
Asante Sana	Thank you very much
Mama	Mother
Baba	Father
Ndada	Sister
Ndugu	Brother
Watoto	Children
Mtoto	Child
Mwalimu	Teacher
Mwanafunzi	Student
Shule	School
Yebo	Yes
La	No
Acha	Stop
Nisamehe	Excuse me
Tafadali	Please
Mzuri	Good
Harambee	Pull together
Pamoja Tutashinda	Together we will win
Mzee	Elder
Chakula	Food
Choo	Toilet
Hodi hodi	Hurry
Tutaonana	Good-bye (See you later)

Numbers

Moja	One
Mbili	Two
Tatu	Three
Nne	Four
Tano	Five
Sita	Six
Saba	Seven
Nane	Eight
Tisa	Nine
Kumi	Ten

There are almost five billion people in the world. Nine of every ten people have color. Asians are first and Africans are second. Africans are not the minority. The African triangle shows Africans living in America, the Caribbean, and Africa.

African people have always worn bright colors. Males can be found wearing short or long dashikis. Females often wear a head wrap, called a gele (gala). The female top is called a buba and the bottom is a lapa. One of the royal materials used is kente (kinta) cloth.

God gave everyone good hair. Natural hair is easy to manage and allows you to play and swim. Some African Americans want their hair to look like that of Whites. Cornrows are a special braid design once worn only by African queens.

Every race has holy days. These are days where you remember your past, have parties in the present, and become inspired for the future. Some African American holy days are:

January 15	Rev. Dr. Martin Luther King's Birthday
February	Black Liberation Month (Founded by Carter G. Woodson in honor of Frederick Douglass' birthday)
May 19	Malcolm X's Birthday
August 17	Marcus Garvey's Birthday
Dec. 26 - Jan. 1	Kwanzaa

The food for the parties includes mangos, avocados, plantain, watermelon, millet, okra, yams, blackeye peas, seafood, and chicken curry.

African people have given their gift of music to the world. They have excelled in gospel, jazz, blues, classical, reggae, rhythm, and pop music. Some of the best known include W.C. Handy, Billie Holiday, Duke Ellington, Leontyne Price, Aretha Franklin, Bob Marley, Stevie Wonder, and Wynton Marsalis. Paul Robeson was one of the best; besides being a lawyer and an athlete, he could sing, act and was committed to African liberation.

African people were the first to write using hie-
roglyphics. Phillis Wheatley was one of the first
African writers in America. The Harlem Renaissance had some of the greatest African American
writers. Langston Hughes wrote:

My people
The night is beautiful,
And so the faces of my people.
The stars are beautiful,
So the eyes of my people
Beautiful, also is the sun
Beautiful, also, are the souls of my people.

Useni Eugene Perkins wrote:

Hey Black Child
Hey Black Child
Do ya know who ya are
Who ya really are
Do ya know you can be
What ya wanna be
If ya try to be
What ya can be
Hey Black Child
Do ya know where ya goin
Where ya really goin
Do ya know you can learn
What ya wanna learn
What ya can learn
Hey Black Child
Do ya know ya are strong
I mean really strong
Do ya know you can do
What ya wanna do
If ya try to do
What ya can do
Hey Black Child
Be what ya can be
Learn what ya must learn
Do what ya can do
And tomorrow your nation
Will be what ya want it to be

Bibliography

Children

Feelings, Muriel. *Moja Means One.* New York: New American Library, 1971.

_____. *Jambo Means Hello.* New York: New American Library, 1974.

Perkins, Useni Eugene. *When You Grow Up.* Chicago: Black Child Journal, 1982.

Thomas, Valerie. *Accent African.* New York: Co - Bob, 1973.

Yarborough, Camille. *Cornrows.* New York: Coward-McCann, 1979.

Adults

Bell, Roseann, edited. *Sturdy Black Bridges.* New York: Anchor Press, 1979.

Chapman, Abraham, edited. *Black Voices.* New York: New American Library, 1968.

Jones, Nathan. *Sharing the Old, Old Story.* Winona: St. Mary's Press, 1982.

Karenga, Maulana. *Kwanzaa.* Los Angeles: Kawaida Publications, 1977.

Vocabulary

Write the definition of each word.

Write a sentence using each word.

Draw a picture of your favorite word on the list or in the chapter.

believe	jazz	native
blood	land	past
church	language	present
culture	liberate	queen
flag	minority	value
future	music	world
holy	nation	write

Questions

1). What is culture?
2). What is a major part of African culture?
3). What are the colors of the Liberation Flag and what do they mean?
4). Why is your native language important?
5). Who is the minority in the world?
6). How do you say hello in Swahili?
7). Who was Paul Robeson?
8). What are cornrows?
9). When is Marcus Garvey's birthday?
10). Name some entertainers that are active in African liberation issues.
11). How would you dress and what would you eat on an African holy day?

Exercises

1). Review African history through music starting with Quincy Jones' "Roots," Ella Jenkins' "Jambo," Kumbaya Johnson's "Lift Every Voice and Sing," Stevie Wonder's "Happy Birthday," Nina Simone's "Young, Gifted, and Black," "Run DMC's Black History Rap," and Gary Byrd's "You Wear the Crown."
2). Write a poem about how beautiful it is to be Black.
3). Make a liberation flag out of construction paper.
4). Have a party, bring African food, and wear African dress.
5). Celebrate Kwanzaa in class.

Chapter Seven

Lessons from History

History should not keep you in the past, it should be joined with the present and future.

We should learn lessons from history. Repeating mistakes should be avoided. Strengths should be remembered.

In order to be free, Africans must understand how they were made slaves. Before Africans went to slave owners, they were "seasoned" by slave makers. Slave makers had to do four things to make a good slave.

1. Place fear in slaves by beating them or killing one publicly as an example.
2. Teach them to be loyal and identify with the owner, by giving traitors favors.
3. Teach them to feel inferior by showing White people in power.
4. Teach them to hate Africa and anything black, by saying harsh words and giving special favors to light-skinned Africans.

Fear

Queen N'Zinga, Harriet Tubman, Malcolm X, Martin Luther King, Jr., and many others were great because they were not afraid of death.

Lesson: If you are not prepared to die for something, you are not fit to live for anything.

Loyalty

Many slave revolts were stopped because slaves told the owners. When Europeans came to Africa they were trusted. Toussaint L'Ouverture trusted the French when he met with them.

Lesson: We must be careful who we trust inside or outside the race—being Black is more than just how you look, but how you think and act.

Inferior

Many history texts list Greece as the origin of civilization. "His - story" means people often tell *their* story rather than the truth. Columbus did not discover America, and Hippocrates is not the father of medicine.

Lesson: Be proud of your history, remember your ancestors built the first civilization. Africans were the first to write, compute, build great buildings, and believe in one God. Because your ancestors were great, you can be also.

Color

When Europeans raped African women to make slave babies, these children were light-skinned. The owner gave light-skinned children more favors. This created jealousy between light-skinned children, who mostly worked in the owner's house and dark-skinned children, who primarily worked in the field.

Many African Americans today do not like dark skin, believe "good hair" is long and straight, pretty eyes are blue or green, and good looking is having light-skin.

Lesson: If having color is negative, why do Whites risk skin cancer trying to get a sun tan? The more color you have, the more that aging will be delayed. The more color you have, the more sun you take in for vitamin D and brain cell development. Good hair is clean, natural hair that allows air in, prevents lice, and allows you to sweat and swim.

Mistake

Africans are very loving people. They want peace with everyone. When the invaders came along the coast, they were treated as friends.

Africans trusted them.

Lesson: Look for the good in everyone, but never turn your back. Avoid the mistakes we made allowing Whites to occupy the coast, and Toussaint trusting France.

Mistake

Human beings are the smartest animals on the planet. Humans can use their brains to develop or destroy the world. Africans used their resources to build pyramids. Europeans used their resources to make guns.

Lesson: If you value what you have, be prepared to defend it.

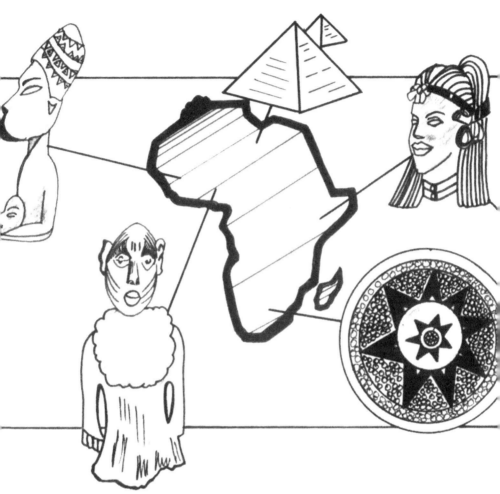

Mistake

When Europeans came to Africa, they saw a lack of racial unity. Africans were divided into 1000 communities. They also spoke over 2,000 languages. Europeans had smaller numbers, but greater unity. For example, if there are 100 unified Europeans fighting 500 Africans divided into 10 groups, who will win?

Lesson: Racial unity is more important than community differences.

Mistake

Africans placed great trust in their leaders. When Arabs and Europeans invaded, they saw kings had great power.

In America, Africans placed great trust in Douglass, Washington, Garvey, Muhammad, Malcolm, and King, but when these men died, the movement slowed down. The leaders were mostly men and primarily from the church.

Lesson: Leaders should come from all groups, not just the church, and women should be included. We should separate the message from the *messenger,* because the latter dies, but the message continues. The message for liberation includes owning businesses, land, schools, believing in self-defense, boycotts, marches, non-violence, and equal opportunity.

Mistake

African Americans have given much to American industry. They invented many things including the shoe lasting machine, telephone transmitter, third rail, carbon filaments, clock, lawn mower, stove, refrigerator, lubricator, soap, ink, and shampoo. It was hard for Africans to protect their inventions because of slavery, lack of money, cheating, and not having faith to start their own businesses.

Lesson: Africans must make business as important as religion, politics, and education. The African community has many churches, politicians, and educators, but very few employers.

Strength

African Americans have done well whenever they were given a chance. Benjamin Banneker just wanted a chance to write an almanac, design Washington, and make a clock.

The Tuskegee Airmen just wanted a chance to fly.

Jackie Robinson just wanted a chance to hit, run, and field.

Lesson: Africans are not just good at sports and music, but are good at whatever they are given a chance to do.

Strength

Africans have always had a love for education. The Grand Lodge of Wa'at was the first university.

Africans risked death during slavery trying to read under a candle or moonlight. After slavery, many Africans created independent Black schools. Mary McLeod Bethune is the founder of Bethune College.

The Black colleges, Council of Independent Black Institutions, and the Clara Muhammad schools are fine examples.

Lesson: Always value education. No one can control a person who knows his identity, purpose, and direction. We are an African people, whose purpose is the liberation of our race, through the Nguzo Saba African Value System.

Strength

Africans have always valued family.

The African proverb, "Children are the reward of life," reflects the love for children.

Africans' respect for elders is shown by placing them as advisors to the community. Husbands and wives risked death and looked out for each other during slavery. This shows the love for family.

Lesson: Long-term happiness is not found in toys, bikes, and clothes, but in the company of family.

Strength

Africans have survived the worst form of slavery ever placed on a people.

Africans' religion, belief in God, and the church saved them.

Africans commit suicide less often than any other race because of their faith.

The African American church is the strongest group in the community.

Lesson: Africans must use their belief and the church beyond survival and use it to promote growth and liberation.

Strength

Africans are very brave people. African Americans have fought in every American war in hopes they too would be free. Africans have fought on the front line and in the boxing ring.

Muhammad Ali also fought a war in court.

Lesson: Before you fight a war for others, fight for freedom for your people.

Strength

There have always been a few Africans whose spirits were never broken. They never forgot Africa and the beauty of being Black. They led the slave revolts.

They refused to move to the back of the bus.
They marched, boycotted, and sat at the lunch counters. They gave speeches, wrote books, and opened schools.

Lesson: The future of the race depends upon those who will carry the torch.

* * * * *

Will you carry the torch for justice, freedom, and liberation?

I hope this book has helped you gain knowledge of your history and has made you proud.

I hope it will inspire you to academic achievement that would make Imhotep proud.

I hope that you will become disciplined, serious, and feel a responsibility to contribute to your race.

Your brother,
Jawanza Kunjufu

Bibliography

Children
Church, Vivian. *Colors Around Me.* Chicago: Afro-Am Publishing, 1971.

Adult
Karenga, Maulana. *Introduction to Black Studies.* Los Angeles: Kawaida Publications, 1982.
Stampp, Kenneth. *The Peculiar Institution.* New York: Vintage, 1956.

Vocabulary

Write the definition for each word.
Write a sentence using each word.
Draw a picture of your favorite word on the list or in the chapter.

avoid	hate
basic	jealous
boxing	mistake
brain	negative
chance	protect
claim	respect
compute	rich
create	risk
delay	save
discover	squeal
elder	start
favor	strength
fear	torch
form	trust
group	worst

Questions

1). Why should we learn history?
2). What are the four key words slave makers used in making slaves?
3). What made some of our people great?
4). What are good reasons to have darker skin?
5). What are good reasons for having natural hair?
6). What did Africans and Europeans use their resources to make?

7). Why were Europeans able to win in Africa?

8). What were some of the messages from the messengers?

9). Why don't Africans own more businesses with the inventions they made?

10). What did Africans love and value?

11). What saved Africans?

12). What did Muhammad Ali teach us?

13). Make two columns. List the mistakes and strengths of our people.

14). Will you carry the freedom torch?

Exercises

1). Listen to Martin Luther King's taped speech, "I've been to the mountain top" and talk about fear.

2). Pair the children off in twos and have each tell the other person why he or she looks good.

3. Write a play and include some African mistakes and strengths.

4. Divide the class into groups of five. Have each group make a list of things that they could make or do that could become a business.

5. Have students write letters to their ancestors, thanking them for all they went through, so that everyone might live a better tomorrow.

6. Let the children choose the various "messages" of liberation and conduct a debate.

7. Make up two cards for each personality mentioned in the book and play the game "Concentration".

8. With one of each card show the card and have students describe the person.

9. Design a poster chart of famous African-Americans and let students recognize each personality.

Index

PLEDGE TO PARENTS

Thank you for bringing me into this world.
I look to you for love, guidance and wisdom.
You are my first and best role model.
I will do what you tell me to do.
I will always respect you.
All I ask, is that you understand,
I'm a child trying to grow in a world
Not fit for children.

JAWANZA KUNJUFU

PLEDGE FROM PARENTS

Thank you for coming into this world.
I will always love you and give you positive direc-
tion.
I understand I am your role model
And you're watching everything I do.
I will listen to you with respect.
All I ask, is that you understand
That before I was blessed with you
I had never been a parent.

JAWANZA KUNJUFU

SCHOOL SETS

Children's Library (best collection of Black children's books ever assembled), Grades K-8, 260 books, SECL . . . $2,799.95
Black History Curriculum Basic Set (SETCLAE), 67 books, teachers' manual, and other products, (*specify grade*), SEBH . . . $679.95 each
Complete Set (SETCLAE), 190 books, 230 posters, 12 videos, 5 games and puzzles and much more! *(specify grade)*, SEC . . . $2,979.00
President Obama Set of 60 books and 3 posters: Obama Set . . . $749.95 *(free shipping)*
Educators' Library 28 books, SEEDL . . . $299.95
Hip Hop Street Curriculum: Dropout Prevention/Motivation 80 assorted books and teachers' manual, (*specify grade*, grades 5-H.S.), *HHST* . . . $799.95 each
Male In-house School Suspension 50 books, *(specify grade)*, SEM . . . $399.95 each
Female In-House School Suspension 50 books, *(specify grade)*, SEF . . . $399.95 each
Black History & Cultural Videos (10 Pack, VHS Only), MIV1 . . . $199.95
Hispanic History & Culture 50 books plus posters, HHCV . . . $419.95
Posters Set (230), SECP . . . $399.99 (non-returnable unless damaged)
Biographies set of 25 Famous African Americans Paperback, BI01 . . . $349.95
Biographies set of 16 Famous African Americans Paperback, BI02 . . . $159.95
Parent Set 28 books SECPA . . . $299.95
Math Set (Elementary), 30 books, 2 videos, and 2 games, SEMA-EL . . . $599.95
Math Set (High School), 30 books, 5 videos, 1 game . . ., SEMA-HS . . . $599.95
Respect/Manners/Home Training 25 books (Hispanic K-8, Biographies 4-12, Character 4-12 and Classics 6-12), RMH-SET . . . $199.95
Best Books for Boys/Girls: Motivational Reading Books for At-risk Males & Females (20 Books), *(specify gender and grade):* SEMR . . . $299.95
Character Developing Books for Youth Set (10 elementary books), CD400 . . . $129.95
H.S. Classics Set of 20 famous black books, CL500 . . . $279.95
Map Set of 10 maps of Africa and the world . . . $299.95
High School Motivation Set of 18 books . . . $209.95
Pre-School Basic Set of 20 books . . . $159.95
Pre-School Complete Set of 60 books, 3 videos, 2 cd's and 2 dolls . . . $669.95
Black History Games (5) and **Black History Puzzles** (5) . . . $199.95
Complete School Set 556 children and adult books, 20 audios and 10 videos: SCHSET . . . $20,699.95

Free Shipping! (for a limited time only)
Don't let your grant monies expire.